C000015948

FRIES

FRIES

DELICIOUS RECIPES FOR CLASSIC, CRUMBED AND TOPPED POTATO AND VEGGIE FRIES, PLUS DIPS

LAURA WASHBURN PHOTOGRAPHY BY STEVE PAINTER

RYLAND PETERS & SMALL
LONDON • NEW YORK

DESIGN, PHOTOGRAPHY AND PROP STYLING Steve Painter
COMMISSIONING EDITOR Nathan Joyce
PRODUCTION MANAGER Gordana Simakovic
ART DIRECTOR Leslie Harrington
EDITORIAL DIRECTOR Julia Charles
PUBLISHER Cindy Richards
FOOD STYLIST Lucy McKelvie
INDEXER Vanessa Bird

First published in 2015 by
Ryland Peters & Small
20–21 Jockey's Fields
London WC1R 4BW
and
341 E 116th St
New York, NY 10029
www.rylandpeters.com
10 9 8 7 6 5 4 3 2 1

ISBN: 978-1-84975-658-7

A CIP record for this book is available from the British Library.

US Library of Congress cataloging-in-Publication Data has been
applied for.

Printed in China

NOTE

*Many of the recipes include cooking with hot oil, so care must
be taken. Please see page 8 for safety information.

CONTENTS

INTRODUCTION

A SIMPLE SLIVER OF POTATO IMMERSED IN BUBBLING OIL – WHAT IS NOT TO LIKE? VERY LITTLE, AS THE UNIVERSAL POPULARITY OF FRENCH FRIES DEMONSTRATES. PEOPLE HAVE THEIR OWN PREFERENCES, FOR THICK-CUT OR THINLY SLICED FRIES, WITH OR WITHOUT THE POTATO SKIN, AND THEN THERE'S THE ARRAY OF DIPS AND SAUCES TO CHOOSE FROM. EVERYONE HAS THEIR OWN SPECIAL COMBINATION.

But who made the first French fry? No one really knows for certain, although they are thought to herald from either France or Belgium. The French story tells us that they were first sold by street vendors on the Pont Neuf in Paris, around the time of the 1789 Revolution. Belgians contest this, with one story claiming that potatoes were deep-fried before 1680 in the Meuse valley.

In any case, it is only in the United States that deep-fried potato slices have a French connection. In Belgium, they're called 'fries' or 'friet' (there's even a Frietmuseum in Bruges, which describes itself as 'the first and only museum dedicated to potato fries'), while in the Netherlands, they're called 'patat' and in France, 'les frites'. In the UK, they are called 'chips', and are doused with malt vinegar and served alongside battered fried fish and mushy peas.

What is beyond doubt is that everyone enjoys a French fry, and they can be enjoyed in a paper cone from a street vendor, or on a porcelain plate alongside a good steak. Eat them with your fingers, a small wooden fork, or with fine cutlery and enjoy them simply salted, drowned in Dutch fashion with satay sauce, mayo and chopped onions, or beneath a Korean-style beef and kimchi topping.

And while potatoes are the obvious choice, they are not the only ingredient that can be sliced and plunged into hot oil. Most root vegetables take kindly to this preparation, and this book includes recipes for more than just potato-based fries. More delicate vegetables, like celeriac and asparagus, get treated to a light crumb coating as well, and for the health-conscious, there is the occasional oven-baked recipe too. Something for everyone, and every occasion.

EQUIPMENT & TECHNIQUES

FRYING CAN BE PERFORMED WITH A FEW SIMPLE PIECES OF EQUIPMENT:

DEEP FRYER

If you use a deep fryer, simply follow the manufacturer's instructions for filling it with oil and heating to temperature.

ON THE STOVETOP

You don't need a deep-fryer – the same results can be achieved with a few ordinary kitchen utensils and a heavy-bottomed saucepan with a depth of at least 10 cm/ 4 inches. It should be wide enough to allow a small batch of fries to be submerged.

COOKING THERMOMETER

A basic cooking thermometer that can be held upright in the middle of the pan will suffice. If you don't have one, test the oil temperature by adding a small cube of bread to the pan; it will turn golden in 10 seconds when the oil reaches 190°C (375°F), the ideal temperature for most of these recipes.

SLOTTED SPOON OR FRYING BASKET

To remove the fries, use an implement that lifts them out of the oil and allows them to drain over the pan for a few seconds. The handle should be long enough to keep your arm well away from spatters.

WHICHEVER FRYING METHOD YOU CHOOSE, THE FOLLOWING TECHNIQUES ALL APPLY:

TYPES OF OIL

Sunflower, peanut, soybean and vegetable oil are all neutral in flavour and have a high smoke point (the temperature at which the oil starts to break down and emit smoke), which makes them all good for frying.

ENSURE THAT THE FOOD IS DRY

Moisture on the food will cause the oil to spatter, so be sure to dry ingredients well before adding to the oil. The exception is for certain recipes that call for a light coating of cornflour/cornstarch paste.

DRAINING

Be sure to allow the food to drain on paper towels to absorb excess surface oil.

SAFETY TIPS

Deep-frying requires supervision and care and so be sure to keep an eye on the temperature of the oil. In the event of a grease fire, do not attempt to carry the pot; use a fire blanket, a damp towel or a fire extinguisher designed specifically for grease fires to suffocate the flames. Be sure to turn off the heat source as well. Never throw water on a grease fire as it will simply add fuel to the fire.

CLASSIC FRIES

THE SIMPLICITY OF HOT, CRISPY POTATOES REQUIRES NOTHING MORE THAN SOME SEA SALT FLAKES AS SEASONING. IF YOU DO WANT A BIT OF A FLOURISH, MALT VINEGAR, MAYONNAISE OR KETCHUP WILL DO THE TRICK. EATING DOES NOT GET MUCH BETTER.

3–4 large floury potatoes, all roughly the same size

vegetable or sunflower oil

sea salt flakes

SERVES 4 AS A SIDE

Peel the potatoes and trim on all sides to get a block. Cut the block into slices about 1-cm/⅜-in. thick, then cut the slices again to get chips.

Put the potatoes into a bowl of iced water for at least 5 minutes, to remove excess starch and prevent sticking when frying.

Fill a large saucepan one-third full with the oil or, if using a deep-fat fryer, follow the manufacturer's instructions. Heat the oil to 190°C (375°F) or until a cube of bread browns in 30 seconds.

Drain the potatoes and dry very well. Working in batches, fry about a handful of potatoes at a time. Place the potatoes in a frying basket (or use a slotted metal spoon) and lower into the hot oil carefully. Fry for 4 minutes. Remove and drain on paper towels. Repeat until all of the potatoes have been fried.

Just before serving, skim any debris off the top of the cooking oil and reheat to the same temperature.

Fry as before, working in batches, but only cook until crisp and golden, about 2 minutes. Remove and drain on paper towels. Repeat until all of the potatoes have been fried.

Sprinkle with the salt flakes and serve.

MATCHSTICK FRIES WITH SICHUAN PEPPER SALT

SUPER-SKINNY AND DELICATE, MATCHSTICKS ARE AN UPMARKET VERSION OF FRIES, SO SERVE THEM FOR YOUR NEXT SPECIAL MEAL. THEY'RE ESPECIALLY NICE WITH VENISON OR VERY GOOD STEAK.

2 large floury potatoes, roughly the same size

vegetable or sunflower oil

cornflour/cornstarch

SICHUAN PEPPER SALT

1 tablespoon Sichuan peppercorns

2 tablespoons coarse rock salt

SERVES 4 AS A SIDE

For the Sichuan Pepper Salt, heat the peppercorns in a small frying pan/skillet until hot but not smoking. Transfer to a plate to cool. Combine with the salt and grind in a spice mill or with a pestle and mortar. Set aside.

Peel the potatoes and trim on all sides to get a block. Cut the block into thin slices, then cut the slices thinly into matchsticks.

Put the potatoes into a bowl of iced water for at least 5 minutes, to remove excess starch and prevent sticking when frying. Put the cornflour/cornstarch in a shallow bowl.

Fill a large saucepan one-third full with the oil or, if using a deep-fat fryer, follow the manufacturer's instructions. Heat the oil to 190°C (375°F) or until a cube of bread browns in 30 seconds.

Drain the potatoes and dry very well, then toss to coat lightly with the cornflour/cornstarch. Put in a sieve/strainer to help shake off any excess cornflour/cornstarch.

Working in batches, fry about a handful of potatoes at a time. Place the potatoes in a frying basket and lower into the hot oil carefully. Fry for about 5 minutes. Remove and drain on paper towels. Repeat until all of the potatoes have been fried.

Sprinkle with the Sichuan Pepper Salt and serve.

GARLIC & HERB POTATO WEDGES WITH GARLIC LEMON MAYO

THE SMELL OF ROASTING GARLIC AND ROSEMARY INFUSES THESE POTATO WEDGES WITH SUNNY MEDITERRANEAN FLAVOURS. TO KEEP THE GOOD FEELINGS GOING, SERVE WITH A GARLIC LEMON MAYO DIP AND IT WILL SEEM LIKE SUMMER, NO MATTER WHAT THE WEATHER.

800 g/1¾ lbs. floury potatoes, preferably Cyprus, scrubbed

4–5 tablespoons vegetable oil

1 teaspoon fine salt

2 garlic cloves, crushed

1 teaspoon dried rosemary

1 teaspoon dried thyme

salt and freshly ground black pepper

GARLIC LEMON MAYO

125 g/1 cup plus 1 tablespoon mayonnaise

2 garlic cloves, crushed

freshly squeezed juice of ½ lemon

SERVES 4-6 AS A SIDE

Preheat the oven to 200°C (400°F) Gas 6. Line a large baking sheet with parchment paper.

In a small bowl, combine the mayonnaise, garlic and lemon juice and stir to mix. Set aside.

Cut the potatoes in half lengthwise, then into thirds so you end up with six long wedges. Put the wedges in a large mixing bowl and add the oil, salt, garlic, herbs and a generous grinding of pepper. Toss well with your hands to coat evenly, then transfer to the prepared sheets and spread evenly in a single layer.

Roast for 20 minutes in the preheated oven, then turn the potatoes and continue roasting for another 10–15 minutes, until deep golden and cooked through. Sprinkle with salt and more pepper and serve with the garlic lemon mayo.

TRUFFLE FRIES

THESE ARE HIGH-CLASS FRIES TO BE SURE, SO SERVE THESE WITH SOMETHING OF EQUAL STANDING, LIKE FILLET STEAK. TO GET THE BEST TRUFFLE TASTE, USE A VERY GOOD BRAND OF TRUFFLE OIL.

2 kg/4½ lbs. floury potatoes, all roughly the same size, peeled

vegetable or sunflower oil

1–2 tablespoons high-quality truffle oil

sea salt flakes

SERVES 4 AS A SIDE

Use a potato chipper to cut the potatoes into strips. Alternatively, cut by hand. Peel the potatoes and trim on all sides to get a block. Cut the block into slices about 1-cm/⅜-in. thick, then cut the slices again to get chips.

Put the cut potatoes into a bowl of ice-cold water for at least 5 minutes, to remove excess starch and prevent sticking when frying.

Fill a large saucepan one-third full with the oil or, if using a deep-fat fryer, follow the manufacturer's instructions. Heat the oil to 190°C (375°F) or until a cube of bread browns in 30 seconds.

Drain the potatoes and dry very well. Working in batches, fry about a handful of potatoes at a time. Place the potatoes in a frying basket and lower into the hot oil carefully. Fry for 3–4 minutes. Remove and drain on paper towels. Repeat until all of the potatoes have been fried.

Just before serving, skim any debris off the top of the cooking oil and reheat to the same temperature.

Fry as before, working in batches, but only cook until crisp and golden, about 2 minutes. Remove and drain on paper towels. Repeat until all of the potatoes have been fried.

Toss with 1 tablespoon of the truffle oil, sprinkle with the salt flakes and taste. Add more oil if desired, then serve immediately.

RUSTIC STEAK FRIES

COARSE-CUT AND WITH THEIR SKINS ON, THESE ARE ROUGH, READY AND TASTY, TOO. SOMETHING ABOUT THEIR SIZE MEANS THEY MARRY WELL WITH POWERFUL FLAVOURS, SO IT'S A GOOD IDEA TO USE STRONG SPICES OR DIPS. THE SEASONING MIX HERE IS BASED ON A POPULAR AMERICAN SEASONING SALT AND IS AN EXCELLENT ALL-ROUNDER.

3 large floury potatoes, all roughly the same size

vegetable or sunflower oil

SEASONED SALT

2 tablespoons fine salt

1 teaspoon caster/granulated sugar

½ teaspoon celery salt

½ teaspoon paprika

¼ teaspoon ground turmeric

¼ teaspoon onion granules

¼ teaspoon garlic granules

pinch of cayenne pepper

SERVES 4 AS A SIDE

In a small bowl, combine the seasoning ingredients and mix well to blend. Set aside.

Scrub the potatoes well and dry. Cut the potatoes into long thin pieces, not as big as a wedge but not as small as a fry. Do not peel.

Put the potatoes into a bowl of iced water for at least 5 minutes, to remove excess starch and prevent sticking when frying.

Fill a large saucepan one-third full with the oil or, if using a deep-fat fryer, follow the manufacturer's instructions. Heat the oil to 190°C (375°F) or until a cube of bread browns in 30 seconds.

Drain the potatoes and dry very well. Working in batches, fry about a handful of potatoes at a time. Place the potatoes in a frying basket and lower into the hot oil carefully. Fry for 4 minutes. Remove and drain on paper towels. Repeat until all of the potatoes have been fried.

Just before serving, skim any debris off the top of the cooking oil and reheat to the same temperature.

Fry as before, working in batches, but only cook until crisp and golden, about 2 minutes. Remove and drain on paper towels. Repeat until all of the potatoes have been fried. Serve with the seasoned salt on the side.

OVEN-BAKED BEETROOT FRIES WITH WASABI MAYO

OPPOSITES ATTRACT, WHICH IS WHY SWEET, ROASTED BEET(ROOT) GOES SO WELL WITH A SPICY JAPANESE WASABI MAYO AND A SESAME-CHILLI SEASONED SALT.

2 kg/4½ lbs. beet(root)

2–3 tablespoons vegetable oil

fine salt

2–3 teaspoons Togarashi (Japanese seven spice) seasoning or black sesame seeds and chilli/hot red pepper flakes

WASABI MAYO

125 g/1 cup plus 1 tablespoon mayonnaise

1 spring onion/scallion, finely sliced

¼ teaspoon wasabi paste, or to taste

SERVES 4 AS A SIDE

In a small bowl, combine the mayonnaise ingredients and mix well to blend. Set aside.

Preheat the oven to 200°C (400°F) Gas 6. Line a large baking sheet with parchment paper.

Scrub the beetroot and trim the ends. Cut into 1-cm/⅜-in. thick slices, and then again into 1-cm/⅜-in. batons.

Transfer to the prepared baking sheet and spread evenly in a single layer. Drizzle over the oil and season lightly with salt. Bake in the preheated oven until tender – around 25–35 minutes.

Remove from the oven and transfer to a serving dish. Sprinkle with the Togarashi seasoning (or black sesame seeds and chilli/hot red pepper flakes) and serve with the mayonnaise for dipping.

NOTE: You can also deep-fry beet(root), by following the method for Sweet Potato Fries on page 23.

SWEET POTATO FRIES WITH CHILLI MAYO

DON'T CUT THESE TOO THIN OR THEY COME OUT ON THE GREASY SIDE – BEST TO GO SLIGHTLY THICK. THE TRICK IS TO PARBOIL TO ENSURE INNER TENDERNESS, COAT LIGHTLY WITH CORNFLOUR/CORNSTARCH TO PROTECT THEM AND THEN JUST FRY BRIEFLY TWICE TO CRISP THEM UP. THE SWEETNESS GOES WELL WITH SPICE, SO PAIR THIS WITH A HOT DIP. I LIKE A CHILLI MAYO.

3 large sweet potatoes

2 tablespoons cornflour/cornstarch

vegetable oil

sea salt flakes

CHILLI MAYO

125 g/1 cup plus 1 tablespoon mayonnaise

½ small fresh red chilli/chile pepper, finely chopped

SERVES 2-4 AS A SIDE

In a small bowl, combine the mayonnaise ingredients and mix well to blend. Set aside.

Scrub the sweet potatoes well. Cut into long thin pieces (about 1.5 cm/⅝ in. long).

Rinse the potatoes and pat dry. Make up a batter with the cornflour/cornstarch and 2 tablespoons water in a shallow bowl. You will need to stir the batter in between coatings; it is also best made in small batches, so keep increasing as needed.

Fill a large saucepan one-third full with the oil or, if using a deep-fat fryer, follow the manufacturer's instructions. Heat the oil to 190°C (375°F) or until a cube of bread browns in 30 seconds.

Working in small batches, dip a handful of sweet potatoes in the cornflour/cornstarch batter, then place in a frying basket (or use a slotted metal spoon) and lower into the hot oil carefully. Fry for 1–2 minutes. Remove and drain on paper towels. Repeat until all of the sweet potatoes have been fried. Just before serving, skim any debris off the top of the cooking oil and reheat to the same temperature.

Coat and fry as before, working in batches, but only cook until crisp and golden, about 1–2 minutes. Remove and drain on paper towels. Repeat until all of the potatoes have been fried.

Sprinkle with salt flakes and serve with the chilli mayo.

OVEN-BAKED CELERIAC FRIES WITH HONEY AND THYME

THIS IS A SOPHISTICATED AND CARB-FREE FRENCH-FRY ALTERNATIVE. THE HONEY COMPLEMENTS THE DISTINCTIVE FLAVOUR OF THIS SUBTLE, NUTTY-TASTING ROOT VEGETABLE AND ALSO HELPS TO GIVE IT A DEEP CARAMEL COLOUR AS IT BAKES.

30 g/2 tablespoons unsalted butter

1 generous tablespoon clear honey

1–2 tablespoons vegetable oil

1 large celeriac

1 small bunch fresh thyme

salt and freshly ground black pepper

SERVES 2-4 AS A SIDE

Preheat the oven to 200°C (400°F) Gas 6. Line a large baking sheet with parchment paper.

Combine the butter and honey in a small saucepan and melt over a low heat. Alternatively, melt in the microwave. Stir in 1 tablespoon of the oil and set aside.

Remove the skin from the celeriac with a small knife, or use a vegetable peeler. Cut the celeriac into 1-cm/⅜-in. thick slices, and then again into 1-cm/⅜-in. batons.

Immediately put the celeriac fries into a large bowl, add the butter mixture and toss well to coat. Add a bit more oil if there is not enough. Season with salt, then transfer to the prepared baking sheet and spread evenly in a single layer. Scatter over the thyme sprigs and bake in the preheated oven until browned – around 25–35 minutes.

Remove from the oven, season lightly with salt and pepper and serve at once.

COATED & CRUMBED

AVOCADO FRIES WITH SOUR CREAM DIP

GLUTEN-FREE BREADCRUMBS HAVE A VERY FINE TEXTURE AND MAKE A FANTASTIC COATING, PERFECT FOR ENCASING VELVETY RICH WEDGES OF AVOCADO.

2 ripe but firm avocados

200 g/4 cups gluten-free breadcrumbs

50 g/3 tablespoons self-raising/rising flour

½ teaspoon fine salt

½ teaspoon paprika

2 eggs

lime wedges, to serve

SOUR CREAM & CHIPOTLE DIP

150 ml/½ cup plus 1 tablespoon sour cream

½ teaspoon chipotle paste, or to taste

few sprigs fresh coriander/cilantro, finely chopped

zest and freshly squeezed juice of 1 lime

SERVES 2-4 AS A SIDE

Preheat the oven to 200°C (400°F) Gas 6. Line a baking sheet with parchment paper.

Combine the breadcrumbs, flour, salt and paprika in a shallow dish.

Put the eggs in a shallow bowl and beat well.

Peel and pit the avocados, then halve them and cut into crescents.

Working one at a time, dip the avocado slices into the egg wash and let the excess drip off, then coat in the breadcrumb mixture. Arrange in a single layer on the prepared baking sheet as you go. It helps if you use one hand for the egg dip and the other for the breadcrumbs.

Bake in the preheated oven until browned and crisp, about 15 minutes.

Meanwhile, combine the Sour Cream & Chipotle Dip ingredients in a small bowl and stir well. Set aside.

Serve hot, with lime wedges and the dip.

HALLOUMI & ZA'ATAR FRIES

IF EVER THERE WAS A CHEESE THAT IMPROVES WITH COOKING, IT'S HALLOUMI, SO IT WORKS FANTASTICALLY WELL WITH CRISPY FRIES. ENJOY THESE SALTY, SQUEAKY STICKS WITH A RICH BEETROOT, YOGURT & MINT DIP, OR ROLL IT ALL UP IN FLATBREAD WITH SOME CRISP LETTUCE.

400 g/14 oz. halloumi

150 g/1 cup plus 1 tablespoon plain/all-purpose flour

1 tablespoons za'atar spice mix, plus more to serve

vegetable oil

lemon wedges, to serve

Beetroot, Yogurt & Mint Dip (see page 60)

SERVES 2-4 AS A SIDE

Cut the halloumi into 2-cm/¾-in. wide strips.

Combine the flour and za'atar in a shallow bowl and mix well.

Fill a large saucepan one-third full with the oil or, if using a deep-fat fryer, follow the manufacturer's instructions. Heat the oil to 190°C (375°F) or until a cube of bread browns in 30 seconds.

Working in batches, coat the halloumi strips in the flour mixture. Place in a frying basket and lower into the hot oil carefully. Fry until golden, for 3–4 minutes. Remove and drain on paper towels. Repeat until all of the halloumi has been fried.

To serve, mound on a platter and scatter over some za'atar. Serve with lemon wedges and the dipping sauce.

LEMON-PEPPER ASPARAGUS FRIES WITH LEMON DIP

AS ASPARAGUS IS PRACTICALLY SHAPED LIKE A FRENCH FRY TO START, THEY LEND THEMSELVES WELL TO A DUNK IN BEATEN EGG AND A COVERING OF CRISPY CRUMB FOR A SATISFYING AND GUILT-FREE FRY. THE ZIPPY TANG OF LEMON COMPLEMENTS THE ASPARAGUS WELL, SO A CITRUS DIP TO GO ALONGSIDE IS JUST THE THING.

200 g/4 cups panko breadcrumbs

1 tablespoon coarse-ground black pepper

½ teaspoon fine salt

50 g/3 tablespoons self-raising/rising flour

zest of 1 lemon

2 eggs

500 g/18 oz. asparagus spears, trimmed

lemon wedges, to serve

LEMON DIP

150 g/⅔ cup mayonnaise

1 garlic clove, crushed

zest and freshly squeezed juice of 1 lemon

pinch of salt and coarse ground black pepper

SERVES 2-4 AS A SIDE

Preheat the oven to 200°C (400°F) Gas 6. Line a baking sheet with parchment paper.

Combine the panko breadcrumbs, black pepper, salt, flour and lemon zest in a shallow dish long enough to fit the length of the asparagus; a baking dish works well.

Put the eggs in a shallow bowl and beat well.

Working one at a time, dip the asparagus spears into the egg wash and let the excess drip off, then coat in the panko mixture. Arrange the spears in a single layer on the prepared baking sheet as you go. It helps if you use one hand for the egg dip and the other for the breadcrumbs.

Bake until browned and crisp, about 15–20 minutes.

Meanwhile, combine the Lemon Dip ingredients in a small bowl and stir well. Set aside.

Serve hot, with the lemon wedges and the dip.

SWEETCORN-SAGE POLENTA FRIES

THESE GOLDEN POLENTA FRIES, FLECKED WITH SWEET NUGGETS OF CORN KERNELS, GO REALLY WELL WITH GRILLED OR FRIED CHICKEN, BUT THEY ARE ALSO SUBSTANTIAL ENOUGH TO BE SERVED AS A MAIN DISH.

1 tablespoon fine salt

250 g/1½ cups plus 2 tablespoons quick-cook polenta/cornmeal

100 g/¾ cup sweetcorn/corn kernels

2 teaspoons dried sage leaves, crumbled

3 tablespoons grated/shredded Parmesan, plus extra to serve

plain/all-purpose flour

vegetable oil

freshly ground black pepper

Chilli Ketchup (see page 59)

SERVES 4 AS A SIDE

Lightly grease a large baking sheet, about 1.5-cm/⅝-in. deep, with vegetable oil.

In a large saucepan, bring 1.5 litres/quarts water to the boil. Add the salt and stir to dissolve. Lower the heat to very low and begin stirring gently with a wooden spoon. As you stir, pour in the polenta/cornmeal in a steady stream. Continue stirring and add the sweetcorn/corn kernels and sage. Cook for 3 minutes, stirring constantly.

Pour the polenta/cornmeal into the prepared baking sheet and spread out evenly, to the thickness of a French fry. Let cool for 20 minutes, then refrigerate for 1 hour to cool completely.

Invert the chilled polenta/cornmeal onto a clean work surface and cut into 8-cm/3-in. long sticks. Put the flour in a dish.

Fill a large saucepan one-third full with the oil or, if using a deep-fat fryer, follow the manufacturer's instructions. Heat the oil to 190°C (375°F) or until a cube of bread browns in 30 seconds.

Working in batches, lightly coat the polenta sticks in flour. Place in a frying basket and lower into the hot oil carefully. Fry until golden, 3–4 minutes. Remove and drain on paper towels. Repeat until all of the sticks have been fried.

To serve, mound on a platter and sprinkle with Parmesan and freshly ground black pepper. Dunk the fries in a rich, spicy pot of Chilli Ketchup.

AUBERGINE & SUMAC FRIES

THE VELVETY SMOOTH TEXTURE OF AUBERGINE IS THE PERFECT VEHICLE FOR SOME WONDERFUL MIDDLE EASTERN INGREDIENTS: SESAME SEEDS, MINT, SUMAC AND LEMON. ZINGY, ZESTY AND FRESH, SERVE THIS AT LUNCH WITH A SELECTION OF SALADS OR WITH SCRAMBLED EGGS FOR A NEW TWIST ON BRUNCH.

500 g/1 lb. 2 oz. aubergine/eggplant, ends trimmed and cut into 2-cm/¾-in. wide strips

125 g/1 cup rice flour

1 tablespoon sumac, plus extra to serve

2–3 sprigs fresh mint, leaves stripped and very finely chopped

1 teaspoon fine salt

vegetable oil

1 tablespoon toasted sesame seeds

lemon wedges and a few sprigs fresh mint, to serve

Lemon & Tahini Dip (see page 60)

SERVES 2-4 AS A SIDE

A few hours before serving (ideally 2–12 hours), put the aubergine/eggplant in a large bowl and add cold water and some ice to cover. Set a plate on top to weigh the aubergine/eggplant down; it must stay submerged.

When ready to cook, combine the rice flour, sumac, chopped mint and salt in a shallow bowl and mix well.

Fill a large saucepan one-third full with the oil or, if using a deep-fat fryer, follow the manufacturer's instructions. Heat the oil to 190°C (375°F) or until a cube of bread browns in 30 seconds.

Working in batches, transfer the damp aubergine/eggplant to the rice flour mixture and coat lightly. Place in a frying basket and lower into the hot oil carefully. Fry until golden, 3–4 minutes. Remove and drain on paper towels. Repeat until all of the aubergine/eggplant has been fried.

Mound on a platter and scatter over the sesame seeds, some sumac and the mint leaves. Serve with lemon wedges and the dipping sauce.

POLENTA & PARMESAN PARSNIP FRIES

THIS RECIPE WAS GIVEN TO ME BY A FRIEND AND CHEF WHO MAKES IT FOR HIS CHILDREN TO GET THEM OUT OF THE POTATO RUT AND EXCITED ABOUT DIFFERENT VEGETABLES. HE HAS VERY LUCKY CHILDREN!

500 g/1 lb. 2 oz. parsnips

100 g/¾ cup plain/all-purpose flour

2 eggs

50 ml/3 tablespoons whole milk

200 g/1¼ cups polenta/cornmeal

50 g/¾ cup Parmesan, finely grated/shredded

vegetable oil

salt and black pepper

mayonnaise, for dipping

SERVES 2-4 AS A SIDE

Scrub the parsnips well and pat dry thoroughly. Cut each parsnip in half crosswise to get two shorter pieces, then halve lengthwise. If the pieces are thick, cut into quarters lengthwise (the top halves will probably need to be quartered but not the bottoms).

Put the flour on a small plate. Combine the eggs and milk in a small bowl, whisk and set aside. Combine the polenta/cornmeal, Parmesan and a good pinch of salt and pepper on a plate, mix well and set aside.

Bring a large pot of water to the boil, then add the parsnips and cook until just tender but not completely soft. Test by inserting the tip of a knife; you should still get some resistance. Time depends on size but about 5 minutes. Drain.

Coat the parsnip slices in the flour, then dip in the egg mixture and transfer immediately to the polenta/cornmeal mix and coat all over. Set aside and continue until all the pieces of parsnip are coated.

Fill a large saucepan one-third full with the oil or, if using a deep-fat fryer, follow the manufacturer's instructions. Heat the oil to 190°C (375°F) or until a cube of bread browns in 30 seconds.

Working in batches, use tongs or a large wire mesh skimmer and transfer the parsnips to the hot oil carefully. Fry until golden, 3–5 minutes. Remove and drain on paper towels. Repeat until all of the parsnips have been fried. Sprinkle with a bit more salt and serve with mayonnaise.

FULLY LOADED

BLUE CHEESE & BACON FRIES

BLUE CHEESE DRESSING WITH CRISPY BACON IS A CLASSIC AMERICAN SALAD DRESSING. THE TRANSITION TO FRENCH-FRY TOPPING IS SEAMLESS, AND POSSIBLY EVEN BETTER.

Classic Fries (see page 11)

2 slices streaky/fatty bacon

100 g/¾ cup blue cheese, crumbled

handful chopped chives, to serve

BLUE CHEESE BÉCHAMEL

2 slices pancetta or streaky/fatty bacon, finely chopped

50 g/3 tablespoons unsalted butter

60 g/4 tablespoons plain/all-purpose flour

550 ml/1 pint milk

½ teaspoon salt

150 g/1¼ cups blue cheese, crumbled

ground black pepper, to taste

SERVES 4

Prepare and cook the fries following the instructions on page 11.

In a frying pan/skillet over a medium-high heat, fry the 2 slices of streaky/fatty bacon and set aside on paper towels. In the same frying pan/skillet, cook the chopped pancetta or bacon (which will form part of the sauce) until crispy and set aside.

Meanwhile, prepare the rest of the blue-cheese béchamel sauce. Melt the butter in a saucepan. Stir in the flour and cook, stirring constantly, for 1 minute. Pour in the milk in a steady stream, whisking constantly and continue whisking gently until the sauce begins to thicken, 3–5 minutes. Stir in the salt. Remove from the heat and add the cheese and chopped pancetta or bacon, mixing well with a spoon to incorporate. Taste and adjust the seasoning.

To serve, mound the fries on a platter and pour over the blue cheese béchamel sauce. Scatter over the crumbled blue cheese and the chives. Top with the set-aside bacon slices, arranged in a criss-cross pattern. Serve immediately.

CURRY FRIES

THIS IS A BRITISH CHIP-SHOP STAPLE THAT'S HUGELY POPULAR. THE SAUCE IS USUALLY A POWDERED MIX BUT, WHEN MADE FROM SCRATCH, IT DOES ELEVATE THIS WELL ABOVE THE AVERAGE. DEPENDING ON HOW HOT YOU LIKE YOUR CURRY, ADJUST THE CURRY-POWDER HEAT IN THE RECIPE AND IF LOTS OF FIERY CHILLI IS DESIRED, ADD A GOOD PINCH OF CHILLI FLAKES AS WELL. GREAT WITH AN ICE-COLD LAGER.

Classic Fries (see page 11)

CURRY SAUCE

2 tablespoons vegetable oil

1 onion, grated

1 apple, peeled and grated

1 garlic clove, crushed

2-cm/¾-in. piece of fresh ginger, peeled and grated

2 tablespoons medium-hot curry powder

1 teaspoon turmeric

1 teaspoon paprika

2 teaspoons ground cumin

½ teaspoon ground coriander

1 tablespoon plain/all-purpose flour

500 ml/2 cups chicken or

vegetable stock

1 teaspoon Worcestershire sauce

1 tablespoon tomato purée/paste

freshly squeezed lemon juice and/or sugar, to taste

SERVES 4

Prepare the curry sauce. Heat the oil in a large non-stick frying pan/skillet with the onion. Cook over a medium heat, stirring occasionally, until aromatic, 3–5 minutes. Add the apple, garlic, ginger, curry powder, turmeric, paprika, ground cumin and ground coriander and cook, stirring for about 1 minute.

Add the flour, add a splash more oil if it is very dry, and cook, stirring continuously for another 1 minute.

While stirring, gradually pour in the stock and stir until well blended. Bring just to the boil, then lower the heat to a simmer. Stir in the Worcestershire sauce and tomato purée/paste and simmer for 15 minutes. Taste. Depending on preference, add some lemon juice for more acidity or a pinch of sugar to sweeten, or both.

Transfer to a blender and whizz until smooth. Set aside while you prepare the fries, according to the recipe for Classic Fries on page 11.

To serve, reheat the curry sauce. Mound the fries on a platter and pour over the sauce. Serve immediately.

POUTINE

THIS IS A MONTREAL CLASSIC, AND IT'S EASY TO SEE WHY, IF YOU THINK ABOUT THE WINTER WEATHER THERE. A PORTION OF FRIES WITH GRAVY AND CHEESE IS JUST WHAT YOU NEED WHEN AN ICY WIND BLOWS IN OFF THE ST LAWRENCE RIVER. IF YOU CAN'T FIND CURD CHEESE, HALLOUMI WILL GIVE A SIMILAR SQUEAKY TEXTURE AND MILD TASTE, OTHERWISE TRY STRING CHEESE OR EVEN CUBES OF MONTEREY JACK.

Classic Fries (see page 11)

300 g/10½ oz. curd cheese, or thinly sliced halloumi

FOR THE GRAVY

1 shallot, very finely chopped

4 tablespoons unsalted butter

30 g/2 tablespoons plain/all-purpose flour

500 ml/2 cups beef stock, hot

500 ml/2 cups chicken stock, hot

2 tablespoons tomato ketchup

1 tablespoon malt vinegar

splash of Worcestershire sauce

salt and freshly ground black pepper

SERVES 4

For the gravy, put the shallot and butter in a saucepan and cook over a medium heat until just soft, about 3 minutes.

Add the flour and cook, stirring constantly, for 1 minute. Add the remaining ingredients and cook, stirring continuously, until the gravy comes to a boil. Lower the heat and continue cooking, stirring continuously, until thick, about 5 minutes more. Taste and adjust seasoning. Set aside while you make the fries.

Prepare and cook the fries following the instructions on page 11.

Reheat the gravy. To serve, divide the fries between four bowls and then add the cheese. Pour over the hot gravy and serve immediately.

CHILLI FRIES

THIS IS A BURGER-JOINT CLASSIC THAT DATES BACK TO MY CHILDHOOD. IT IS MESSY, SUBSTANTIAL AND NOT VERY GLAMOROUS, BUT BOY DOES IT TASTE GOOD. THIS IS FRENCH-FRY CUISINE AT ITS FINEST.

1 tablespoon vegetable oil

1 small onion, finely chopped

1 small red (bell) pepper, diced

2 garlic cloves, crushed

400 g/14 oz. minced/ground beef

1 teaspoon ground cumin

1 teaspoon dried oregano

½ teaspoon cayenne pepper, or to taste

1 x 400-g/14-oz. can chopped tomatoes

1 x 400-g/14-oz. can black beans, drained

salt and ground black pepper

Classic Fries (see page 11)

Worcestershire sauce, optional

chilli sauce, optional

Tabasco, optional

125 g/1¼ cups finely grated/

shredded mild cheese, such as Monterey Jack or mild Cheddar

few spoonfuls of sour cream

1 spring onion/scallion, finely chopped

SERVES 4

In a large pot, combine the oil, onion and pepper and cook over a medium heat, stirring occasionally, until soft.

Add the garlic and meat and cook, stirring to break up the pieces, until cooked through. Add the cumin, oregano and cayenne pepper, stir well and cook for 1 minute longer.

Season well with salt and pepper and stir in the tomatoes, fill the tomato can halfway with water, stir and add it, along with the beans. Lower the heat and simmer, covered, for 20–30 minutes.

Prepare and cook the Classic Fries by following the instructions on page 11 while the chilli simmers.

Taste the chilli and adjust the seasoning, adding any sauces as desired.

To serve, mound the fries on a platter and pour over the chilli. Scatter over the cheese, dollop on the sour cream and finish with the spring onions/scallions. Serve immediately.

PEPPERONI PIZZA FRIES

TOMATO SAUCE AND MELTED CHEESE GO WELL ON A BREAD DOUGH BASE SO WHY NOT SERVE THEM ATOP A MOUND OF FRIES? PEPPERONI SLICES HELP THIS ALONG VERY NICELY, BUT ANYTHING THAT WORKS ON A PIZZA WILL WORK HERE, SO PLEASE DO FEEL FREE TO EXPERIMENT WITH TOPPINGS.

Classic Fries (see page 11)

1 tablespoon vegetable oil

1 red onion, halved and thinly sliced

1 teaspoon dried oregano

2 tablespoons balsamic vinegar

200 g/7 oz. passata/strained tomatoes

55 g/2 oz. pepperoni slices, halved if large

50 g/2 oz. stoned/pitted black olives, sliced

350 g/3 cups finely chopped or ready grated/shredded mozzarella

SERVES 4

Prepare and cook the fries following the instructions on page 11.

Meanwhile, heat the oil and fry the onion and oregano in a small frying pan/skillet until soft. Add the balsamic vinegar and cook, stirring, until evaporated. Set aside.

Preheat the grill/broiler to high.

Spread the fries in a shallow baking dish and drizzle the passata/strained tomatoes over, then drop on blobs of the balsamic onion. Scatter over the pepperoni followed by the olives, then top all over with the mozzarella.

Place under the preheated grill/broiler until the cheese melts and just turns golden, about 5 minutes. Serve immediately.

NACHO FRIES

SALSA IS ONE OF LIFE'S LITTLE PLEASURES SO IT SHOULDN'T JUST BE SERVED WITH TORTILLA CHIPS. THIS IS A FRENCH-FRY TWIST ON A TEX-MEX STAPLE AND THE FLAVOURS ALL THRIVE ON THEIR NEW POTATO-BASED HOME. TRY IT AND SEE.

Classic Fries (see page 11)

1 x 400-g/14-oz. can refried beans

350 g/3 cups grated/shredded Monterey Jack or mild Cheddar

1 quantity Salsa (see page 56)

1 quantity Guacamole (see page 56)

100 g/½ cup sour cream

2 spring onions/scallions, thinly sliced

3–4 tablespoons sliced pickled jalapeños, or to taste

SERVES 4

Prepare and cook the fries following the instructions on page 11.

Preheat the grill/broiler to high.

Warm the refried beans in a small saucepan. Consistency varies by brand, so you may need to add a splash of water to make them easier to spoon on; if they're really thick, stir in a spoonful of salsa to help thin without diluting the taste.

Spread the fries on a shallow baking sheet and top with blobs of the beans, spread to cover fairly evenly. Scatter over the cheese in an even layer.

Place under the preheated grill/broiler until the cheese melts, about 5 minutes.

Remove from the oven and top with blobs of salsa, guacamole and sour cream. Scatter over the spring onions/scallions and jalapeños and serve.

KOREAN BBQ KIMCHI FRIES

THIS MAD-GENIUS CREATION EMERGED FROM THE AUSTIN, TEXAS FOOD-TRUCK SCENE. IT TAKES A LITTLE WHILE TO PREPARE, BUT IT'S DEFINITELY WORTH THE WAIT!

Classic Fries (see page 11)

125 g/generous ½ cup mayonnaise

3 tablespoons Sriracha, or other hot sauce, plus more to serve

50 g/¾ cup grated/shredded mild cheese, such as mild Cheddar or Monterey Jack

1 spring onion/scallion, thinly sliced

1 teaspoon toasted sesame seeds

few sprigs fresh coriander/cilantro, finely chopped

BULGOGI

2 spring onions/scallions, thinly sliced

2 garlic cloves, crushed

2 tablespoons sugar

1 tablespoon sesame oil

1 tablespoon vegetable oil

1 tablespoon mirin

125 ml/½ cup soy sauce

500 g/1 lb. 2 oz. beef steak (ribeye, sirloin/New York strip or flank), very thinly sliced

CARAMELIZED KIMCHI

200 g/7 oz. kimchi

100 g/½ cup sugar

60 ml/¼ cup malt vinegar

1 tablespoon gochujang (Korean chilli paste)

1 tablespoon soy sauce

SERVES 4

One day before serving, prepare the bulgogi. Combine all the ingredients in a bowl and toss to coat thoroughly. Transfer to a resealable plastic bag, or a shallow glass dish and cover. Refrigerate for at least 12 hours.

The day of serving, prepare the potatoes according to the recipe for Classic Fries on page 11. Keep warm in an oven set at a low temperature while you prepare the toppings.

In a small bowl, mix the mayonnaise and the Sriracha. Set aside.

For the kimchi, combine all the ingredients in a mixing bowl and toss to coat evenly. Heat a large non-stick frying pan/skillet. When hot, add

the kimchi and cook over a high heat, stirring occasionally, until browned, 3–5 minutes. Remove and set aside.

For the bulgogi, heat the same large non-stick frying pan/skillet. When hot, add the meat and marinade and cook, stirring once or twice, until just seared, 3–4 minutes.

To serve, pile the fries on a platter. Scattter over the kimchi, bulgogi and cheese, then drizzle over the mayo. Top with the spring onion/scallion, sesame seeds and coriander/cilantro. Serve with hot sauce on the side.

DUTCH SATAY FRIES

A STREET FOOD SPECIALITY OF HOLLAND, THIS CREATION PAIRS FRIES WITH A PEANUTTY SATAY SAUCE, MAYO AND DICED RAW ONION. IN DUTCH IT IS CALLED 'PATAJE OORLOG', WHICH MEANS 'WAR FRIES'.

Classic Fries (see page 11)

mayonnaise, for serving

1 onion, diced

SATAY SAUCE

1 tablespoon peanut oil

1 small onion, grated

1 garlic clove, crushed

1-cm/⅜-in. piece of fresh ginger, peeled and grated

2 teaspoon sambal olek (Indonesian chilli/chile paste)

150 g/⅔ cup smooth peanut butter

1 tablespoon soy sauce

1 tablespoon clear honey or brown sugar

500 ml/2 cups chicken or vegetable stock

SERVES 4

Prepare the satay sauce. Heat the oil in a medium non-stick frying pan/skillet with the onion. Cook over a medium heat, stirring occasionally, until aromatic, 3–5 minutes. Add the garlic, ginger and sambal olek and cook, stirring for about 30 seconds. Stir in the peanut butter, soy sauce, honey or brown sugar and stock and stir until well blended. Simmer for 3–5 minutes. If the mixture is very thick, add water or more stock to thin. Taste. Add more soy and/or honey depending on preference. Set aside while you prepare the fries.

Prepare the fries according to the recipe for Classic Fries on page 11.

To serve, gently reheat the satay sauce. Mound the fries on a platter and pour over the sauce, a few dollops of mayo and scatter over the onion. Serve immediately.

BBQ CHICKEN FRIES

CHICKEN, BARBECUE SAUCE AND FRIES OFTEN END UP TOGETHER ON A PLATE, SO THIS COMBO IS OBVIOUS, BUT IT'S THE ADDITION OF MELTED CHEESE THAT ELEVATES IT TO NEW HEIGHTS. A CROWD-PLEASER, FOR SURE.

Classic Fries (see page 11)

300 g/10½ oz. cooked boneless chicken meat, shredded (see Note)

250 ml/1 cup BBQ Sauce (see page 56), plus more for drizzling

salt and freshly ground black pepper

300 g/3 cups grated Red Leicester, or other orange, mild cheese

350 g/12 oz. cheese sauce (follow the Blue Cheese Béchamel sauce recipe on page 39, but substitute grated/shredded Cheddar for the blue cheese)

SERVES 4

Prepare and cook the fries following the instructions on page 11, but undercook slightly, as they bake again to melt the cheese.

Meanwhile, in a saucepan, combine the shredded chicken and the barbecue sauce and warm over a low heat, stirring occasionally. Taste and adjust the seasoning. Set aside and keep warm.

Warm the cheese sauce in another small saucepan. Set aside and keep warm.

Preheat the oven to 200°C (400°F). Spread the fries in a shallow baking dish. Scatter the cheese all over and return to the preheated oven to melt the cheese, about 5 minutes.

Remove from the oven and pour over the warm cheese sauce, then mound the warm chicken on top. Drizzle with extra BBQ sauce and serve.

NOTE: The meat from two leg and thigh portions of a large chicken is about the right amount. For the best texture, poach the chicken. Alternatively, use leftovers from a roast chicken.

TEX-MEX DIPS

GUACAMOLE

2 ripe avocados, pitted and mashed

3–4 tablespoons sour cream

freshly squeezed juice of ½ lemon

small bunch fresh coriander/cilantro, finely chopped

pinch of ground cumin

½ teaspoon fine sea salt

1 small fresh red chilli/chile, finely chopped, optional

Combine all the ingredients in a bowl and mix well. Taste and adjust seasoning, adding more salt or lemon juice as desired. Serve at once.

SALSA

2 fresh green jalapeños

400-g/14-oz. can plum tomatoes

small bunch fresh coriander/cilantro, trimmed

1 small onion, coarsely chopped

1 garlic clove, crushed

good pinch ground cumin

pinch of salt and sugar

freshly squeezed juice of ½ lime

Preheat the oven to 200°C (400°F) Gas 6. Roast the jalapeños until charred and tender, 15–20 minutes. Let cool slightly. Remove the seeds, if desired, for a milder sauce.

Put all the ingredients in a food processor and whizz until almost smooth. Transfer to a bowl and taste for seasoning. Let stand for at least 30 minutes before serving. It will keep, covered, in the refrigerator for at least 5 days.

BBQ SAUCE

500 ml/2 cups tomato ketchup

60 ml/¼ cup malt vinegar

60 ml/¼ cup Worcestershire sauce

50 g/¼ cup dark brown sugar

2 tablespoons clear honey

2 tablespoons mustard powder

¼ teaspoon paprika

¼ teaspoon ground cumin

¼ teaspoon garlic powder

generous pinch chilli/hot red pepper flakes

Combine all the ingredients in a saucepan and bring just to the boil over a medium heat. Reduce the heat to low and simmer for 15 minutes. Taste and adjust the seasoning, adding more salt, vinegar or chilli/hot red pepper flakes to taste. The sauce will keep, covered, in the refrigerator for at least 1 week.

DIPS & SAUCES

KETCHUPS

TOMATO KETCHUP

1 kg/2 lbs. 3 oz. ripe tomatoes, cored and chopped

150 ml/½ cup plus 2 tablespoons vinegar (malt or cider)

50 g/¼ cup soft dark brown sugar

½ teaspoon fine salt

pinch of ground cinnamon

pinch of ground cloves

pinch of celery salt

Put the tomatoes in a saucepan and cook over medium-high heat, stirring occasionally, until they break down, 15–20 minutes. Transfer to a food processor and whizz until smooth, then rub through a fine-mesh sieve/strainer and return the paste to a clean pan. Continue cooking the tomato pulp over a low heat, stirring often, until very thick. Stir in the remaining ingredients and simmer for 5 minutes. Taste and adjust seasoning, adding more vinegar and/or sugar according to taste. The sauce will keep, covered, in the fridge for at least 1 week.

CURRY KETCHUP

1 small onion, grated

2 tablespoons vegetable oil

2 tablespoons curry powder

1 tablespoon hot paprika

½ teaspoon mustard powder

pinch of ground cloves

500 g/1 lb. 2 oz. passata/strained tomatoes

6 tablespoons dark brown sugar

125 ml/½ cup malt vinegar

salt

In a saucepan, soften the onion in the oil, 3–5 minutes. Stir in all the spices and cook until aromatic, about 1 minute more. Add the passata/strained tomatoes, sugar, vinegar and salt to taste. Stir to dissolve and bring to the boil, then lower the heat and simmer until thick like ketchup. Taste and adjust seasoning. The sauce will keep, covered, in the fridge for at least 1 week.

CHILLI KETCHUP

1 small onion, finely chopped

1 tablespoon vegetable oil

1 garlic clove, crushed

700 g/1½ lbs. passata/strained tomatoes

¼ teaspoon chilli/hot red pepper flakes

1 teaspoon tomato ketchup

splash of cider vinegar

salt and freshly ground black pepper

In a saucepan, soften the onion in the oil, 3–5 minutes. Stir in the garlic, passata/strained tomatoes, chilli/hot red pepper flakes and ketchup and bring to the boil, then lower the heat and simmer until thick. Add some salt, pepper and a splash of vinegar; taste and adjust seasoning. It will keep, covered, in the fridge for at least 1 week.

CREAMY DIPS

HARISSA, YOGURT & LEMON DIP

200 g/7 oz. Greek yogurt

1 teaspoon harissa paste

¼ preserved lemon, rind only, finely chopped

pinch of sumac

clear honey, for drizzling

Combine the yogurt, harissa and lemon rind in a bowl and stir to blend. Sprinkle over the sumac and top with a few swirls of honey. Serve.

BEETROOT, YOGURT & MINT DIP

400 g/14 oz. cooked beet(root)

2 tablespoons extra virgin olive oil

6–8 tablespoons Greek yogurt

2 garlic cloves, crushed

pinch of ground cumin

few fresh mint leaves, finely chopped

salt and freshly ground black pepper

In a food processor, combine the beet(root), oil and yogurt and whizz to obtain a coarse dip. Transfer to a bowl and stir in the garlic, cumin and a pinch of salt. Taste and adjust seasoning. Sprinkle with the mint and serve.

LEMON & TAHINI DIP

200 g/7 oz. Greek yogurt

3 tablespoons tahini

1 garlic clove, crushed

freshly squeezed juice of ½ lemon

1 spring onion/scallion, finely chopped

1 teaspoon toasted sesame seeds

clear honey, for drizzling

pomegranate molasses, for drizzling

In a bowl, stir together the yogurt, tahini, garlic, lemon juice and spring onion/scallion. Sprinkle over the sesame seeds and top with a drizzle of honey, followed by a drizzle of pomegranate molasses. Serve.

MAYOS

GREEN GODDESS

200 g/¾ cup plus 2 tablespoons mayonnaise

50 ml/3 tablespoons sour cream

freshly squeezed juice of ½ lemon

2–3 anchovy fillets, finely chopped

small bunch chives, finely chopped

2 sprigs each fresh tarragon, parsley and basil, leaves finely chopped

1 tablespoon capers in brine, drained and finely chopped

1 small garlic clove, crushed

salt and freshly ground black pepper

Tabasco, optional

Combine all the ingredients in a bowl and stir well to blend. Taste and adjust seasoning. Let stand at least 30 minutes before serving.

CHILLI & LIME GARLIC MAYO

250 g/1 cup plus 2 tablespoons mayonnaise

2 garlic cloves, crushed

½ fresh red chilli/chile, deseeded and finely chopped

zest and freshly squeezed juice of 1 lime

Combine all the ingredients in a bowl and mix well. Let stand at least 30 minutes before serving.

TRUFFLE MAYO

250 g/1 cup plus 1 tablespoon fresh mayonnaise

1 tablespoon truffle oil

a few chives, very finely chopped

truffle salt, to taste

Combine the mayonnaise, oil and chives in a bowl and mix well. Let stand at least 30 minutes before serving. Just before serving, dust with a good pinch of truffle salt.

INDEX

What's special about sea lochs?

The scenery alone, with magnificent mountains descending directly into deep, dark sea lochs, or wide basins freckled with islands and skerries, is enough to mark the west coast of Scotland as a very special place. But there is more to the sea loch story. The deep basins, shallow sills, tidal rapids, plunging underwater reefs and sheltered shores of sea lochs make them very unusual, special habitats for a wide variety of marine life.

Each sea loch has its own unique character. Some of the more complex sea lochs, such as Loch Sween or Loch Maddy (which has at least 22 sills) have many arms, each with their own discrete collection of species.

Because the heads of many sea lochs are extremely sheltered from wave action, we can find a variety of marine habitats quite different to those on the open coast; for example, deep sheltered bedrock and plains of fine mud.

Tidal rise and fall varies from between 1 and 5 metres in different parts of the west coast. Fast tidal currents across the narrow sills reach speeds of 8 - 9 knots (15 - 16 kilometres per hour). These tidal rapids and sounds support a thriving diversity of marine life, sustained by a constant supply of food carried by the currents. Rainfall on the west coast of Scotland is notoriously high, with over 1,000mm per year recorded in many places, much of which eventually runs into the sea. On the open coast this freshwater is quickly mixed with seawater by the wind and waves. But in the sheltered sea lochs, where wave action is slight, the less dense freshwater often floats as a discrete layer on top of the seawater.

In a few lochs, particularly at the top end of the arms of some of the fjards in the Western Isles, lagoons are separated from the rest of the loch by a very narrow, shallow entrance sill which only receives seawater around high tide. These lagoons are permanently brackish and support both fresh and sea water animals and plants. These communities have great natural heritage and conservation value, but are highly specialised and not covered further in this booklet.

The diverse habitats within sea lochs are home to a wide range of species. Over 1,700 species have been recorded in the recent survey of the Scottish sea lochs carried out as part of the Marine Nature Conservation Review. There are probably many more as many of the deepest areas have not yet been sampled.

Frozen surface freshwater in Loch Carron